Native American Culture for Kids

The English Reading Tree

Published by G-L-R

Written by Keith Goodman

This book has been written for children aged seven and over, and it is part of the English Reading Tree Series.

Your child will be able to read the majority of words, but those that cause difficulty should be read together and pronounced slowly.

This is the perfect tool for parents to get their children into the habit of reading and focusing them on how words are formulated and used within simple sentences.

If a word does cause difficulties, make sure to re-read the sentence containing it, again, and go through the meaning if necessary.

Here is a fun activity before you start to read

How many things do you know about Native American Culture?

1 Why did European settlers call Native Americans, Indians?

2 What is a reservation?

3 What is the leader of a tribe called?

4 Who was killed at the Little Big Horn?

5 What was the 'Ghost Dance?'

6 How did Geronimo die?

7 Who was the famous chief and medicine man of the Sioux?

8 What happened at Wounded Knee?

Table of Contents

Geronimo

Sitting Bull

Facts and Trivia

How many things have you learned?

European settlers arrive in America

There is not a lot of information about dates and events in the history of Native Americans before the arrival of European settlers.

Christopher Columbus in1492 made the first contact. He thought that he had landed in the East Indies, and that is why he called them Indians.

There were hundreds of tribes scattered throughout America when Columbus landed. A lot of these tribes are well known to us today and include the Navajo, Apache, and Cherokee.

In the following pages, you are going to learn about their culture, their traditions and much more. Scientific experts have used DNA to trace the origins of the Native American population. It is thought that the first American migrants, crossed between Northeast Asia and America through a natural land bridge (Bering Bridge) that existed during the ice age over 15,000 years ago. Northeast Asia is a region that includes China, Japan, North Korea and South Korea.

Native American food and farming

The indigenous people of America got their food by a combination of hunting, fishing, farming and gathering. A lot of what was eaten depended on where a tribe lived.

Sioux Chief

Although most tribes did farming, the most successful came from the southern states because conditions were better. The main crop was corn, but they also cultivated potatoes, pumpkins, beans and squash.

Hunting and fishing provided protein, and buffalo herds were very important. These animals not only provided meat, but also hide for clothes, blankets and shelter, tools and weapons. No part of the animal was wasted. Other animals that were hunted included rabbits, ducks, and deer.

As well as spears, Native Americans used nets to catch fish. The fish were often smoked so they could be preserved during winter months when food was scarce.

The tribes were hunter/gatherers, and they used plants that grew around them. They would gather fruit, nuts, and berries to supplement their diet.

What type of homes did they have?

Native Americans had a broad range of homes. The sort of constructions that were built would depend on the materials available where they lived, and their type of lifestyle.

The tepee was used by tribes that were nomadic. This was a structure that was easy to put up and take down as the tribe moved to another area. This structure was commonly used by the tribes that lived on the Great Plains. These people followed the buffalo herds that roamed the plains.

Other tribes were not nomadic, so they built structures that were permanent.

A wigwam was a structure that was built from wood and was in the shape of a dome. Each wigwam would house a family, although they were very small.

Other shelters that were used included:

- Mud and twig constructions
- Igloos (Alaska)
- Clay and grass houses (Hogan)
- Thatched roofs with open sides (Chickee)

Clothes

The clothes of Native Americans varied according to the climate that they lived in. There were, however, several similarities.

The material most widely used to make clothing was animal hide and fur. Some tribes would also make clothes from plants or weaving cotton thread.

Clothes were handmade by the women in the tribe. These women were very skillful at turning the hide into tough leather and cutting and sewing it together to make garments.

Native Americans loved to decorate clothing with feathers, fur, and porcupine quills.

The men wore a breechcloth. This was material that tucked into a belt and covered their front and back. In colder climates, they wore leggings but usually did not wear shirts. In winter, they would cover up with a cloak.

Women in the tribe wore skirts and leggings. In some tribes, tunics and buckskin dresses were also worn.

Native Americans wore footwear. This was normally a shoe that was created out of soft leather, called a moccasin. In cold places such as Alaska, the people wore a thicker shoe called a Mukluk

Religion

The Native Americans had very strong spiritual beliefs. Nature played a huge role in their everyday lives. Every tribe developed a unique belief system that was passed down the generations using stories and rituals. For all of the tribes, the certainty of the spirit world was vitally important.

Some tribes believed that every living thing had its own guardian spirit, this included plants, people, animals and even mountains and water. Young boys needed to find their guardian spirit before becoming men.

There was a trust in the Great Spirit that watched over everything and everyone.

The tribal spiritual leaders were called medicine men or medicine women. They had the power to heal by calling on the spirit world. They also used special herbs to cure ailments.

Some tribes thought that there were three worlds. Our world, an upper world, and a lower world.

The upper world was pure. The lower world was chaotic and terrifying. It was up to the Native Americans to maintain a balance between these worlds to preserve harmony. This was surprisingly similar to some Asian cultural beliefs.

The tribes celebrated the coming of age passage from being a child to an adult. In some tribes, there were initiation tasks that had to be completed so that a young boy could take his place as a man in the tribe.

To become closer to the spirit world, it was not uncommon for tribal members to go off on their own to see a vision of the spirit world. They thought that the tops of mountains were holy places and often headed for a high place, in search of enlightenment. This would often happen if they had to make a major life changing decision.

The ceremonial pipe of peace was passed around as a way of communicating with the Great Spirit.

Unlike the Ancient Egyptian culture, the Native Americans were not concerned with death and the afterlife. Dying was accepted, and they believed that the afterlife was a happy place with sunny skies and good hunting.

Tribal life

The social structures of the Native American tribes were very important. Laws were passed down verbally, and there were no written rules to be followed. However, every tribe had a clear structure, and there were social rules that had to be obeyed. Anybody who didn't follow the rules would be banished to live outside the tribe.

Cheyenne Family Unit

A tribe was made up of a number of clans. The clans shared a common culture and language. Every clan had a symbol to set it apart from the rest.

These symbols were usually animals or something to do with the environment such as deer, bear, water or mountain.

At the head of each clan was the chief. The chief was elected by his people. A tribe could have a leader chosen especially for war, and another one to guide them in times of peace.

A clan was made up of families that would live together in a village.

Male and female members of a family had different roles to fulfill. The chief was normally a man, but the leader of a family could well be a woman, who played a central role.

Apache

The Apache nation is made up of six tribes. These are the Kiowa, Western Apache. Mescalero, Lipan, Jicarilla and Chiricahua. They lived on the Southern Great Plains in Texas, Arizona, Oklahoma and New Mexico. They are related very closely to the Navajo tribe.

They lived in wigwams and tepees and wore buckskin clothes decorated with feathers, shells, and beads.

Apache warriors with Geronimo on right of picture

The Apache had a staple diet of corn and buffalo meat. They also ate berries, acorns, deer and rabbit. This tribe hunted using the bow and arrow. When they moved their village, they would carry possessions on a travois, which was a kind of sled.

Life in an Apache village was based around the family. The men hunted for food, and the Apache women were responsible for cooking and looking after the home.

At the end of the 1800s, the Apache's had a number of battles against the United States Government to try and keep control of their land. In the end, they were defeated and forced to live on reservations.

Two famous Apache leaders were Geronimo and Cochise.

Today, many Apache tribes still live on reservations in Arizona and New Mexico.

Blackfoot

The Blackfoot consisted of four tribes that were spread over the Great Northern Plains. They followed the huge buffalo herds and were nomadic hunters.

These people were ferocious warriors but suffered greatly from the arrival of white settlers and the overhunting of the buffalo herds.

Blackfoot Chiefs

This caused great hardship for the Blackfoot nation. It eventually led them to be forcibly moved onto reservations in Canada and Montana. These great hunters were forced to take up farming to feed themselves.

The Blackfoot used tepees that could be quickly put up and taken down. This suited their nomadic way of life.

They wore clothes made out of animal hide. The women wore long dresses to protect them from the cold.

The staple diet of the Blackfoot was buffalo, but they also hunted for deer, rabbits, and elk. For the cold winter, they preserved meat by making pemmican. This was a combination of meat, fat and wild berries.

They lived in small mobile clans. Each clan had its own chief.

The origin of the name Blackfoot remains a mystery. Some people think that it comes from the fact that they wore black moccasins.

The four tribes that make up the Blackfoot nation are the northern and southern Piegan, Siksika and Kalian.

Today, there are approximately 32,000 Blackfoot on reservations in the United States and Canada. The largest number live in Montana (7, 0000).

Cherokee

The Cherokee represent the biggest Native American Nation in the United States. The name translated into English means 'speakers of another language.'

These people lived in what is now North Carolina, South Carolina, Alabama, Georgia, and Tennessee. They built homes that were made of wood, grass, and mud (wattle and daub).

The Cherokee were hunter and gatherers but also farmers. They grew beans, squash, and corn, and hunted deer, rabbits, bear and wild turkeys.

Most Cherokee villages were made up of about 30 – 50 families. In the village, the Cherokee women looked after the family and the farming, and the men hunted and protected the community.

Cherokee warrior

Because they lived in the East, they had a lot of contact with the new white settlers. Many treaties were made and broken. The Cherokees fought with the French against the British. When the French lost, the Cherokee Nation was punished by having land taken away.

They lost again during the American War of Independence, by this time siding with the British.

In 1838, the Cherokee were forcibly relocated from their land and moved to Oklahoma. The March of Tears took place in 1838, and more than 4000 died on the trip.

The Cherokee language has a system of writing with an alphabet

Today, there are three recognized Cherokee tribes. These are the Cherokee Nation, the United Keetoowah Band and the Eastern Band

Cheyenne

The Cheyenne lived on the Great American Plains. Today, they have two distinctive clans. The Northern Cheyenne who live on a reservation in Montana, and the Southern Cheyenne in Oklahoma.

Before the arrival of European settlers, the Cheyenne farmed the land in Minnesota. They moved to the Great Plains and began to hunt for buffalo. With the increasing number of settlers, the Cheyenne had a lot of land taken. Despite fighting back, they were eventually forced to move onto a reservation.

Cheyenne Chief Two Moons

The early villages of the Cheyenne were built with permanent dwellings of wood, earth, grass and mud. The Cheyenne of the Great Plains were nomadic so lived in tepees.

The Cheyenne language is unique and has an alphabet consisting of 14 letters.

The men wore breechcloths made from animal hide, and the women wore long dresses. When it was cold in the winter, they had cloaks made from buffalo hide for warmth.

The early Cheyenne farmers grew a lot of crops that included squash, corn, and beans. The Cheyenne of the Great Plains were nomadic and hunted the buffalo for food.

The Cheyenne were friendly with the Sioux and the Arapaho but often fought the Crow and Pawnee.

Chickasaw

The original home of the Chickasaw was in the area that is now called Kentucky, Tennessee, Alabama, and Mississippi. In 1832, the US government forced them to sell their land, and the nation migrated to Oklahoma. The Chickasaw had a reputation for being brave warriors.

Originally, the Chickasaw lived in village communities, in wattle and daub houses. It was usual for the homes to be built in a circle with the center being the meeting place for socializing.

The men wore breechcloths made out of animal skins. The women wore dresses and skirts made out of hide. The Chickasaw men shaved their heads but left a single lock of hair on top. This was called a scalp lock. The women of the tribe tied their hair up using beads.

They were excellent at hunting and farming. They harvested squash, beans, and corn, hunted deer and fished in the rivers and lakes.

The Chickasaw had a well-defined system of government. Each clan had a chief, and they would report to the chief and elders of the whole nation.

After the 1830 Indian Removal Act, the Chickasaw had to move to Oklahoma as part of a massive migration plan. The tribes called it the 'Trail of Tears,' and those who took part, were the Chickasaw, Choctaw, Seminole and the Cherokee.

Cree

The Cree lived in Canada and had two specific groups. The Woodland and the Plains Cree.

Before the arrival of the European settlers, the Cree lived in small clans all over Canada. When the steady stream of European settlers arrived, the Cree adapted and began to trade fur for clothes and horses. As a nation, they were not affected as much by the settlers in the early years. However, the general expansion of the Europeans and the disappearance of the vast buffalo herds had a huge impact. The Cree were eventually forced into controlled reservations.

The Woodland Cree built homes using wood and animal hides. The Cree from the Great Plains favored tepees, which could be put up and pulled down quickly

The Cree were hunter-gatherers. The hunted rabbit, buffalo, elk, duck, and moose. They gathered plants that grew around them, such as wild berries, rice, and turnips.

The Cree had no formal government in place between the various clans. Though each village had a leader, they did not join together to create any formal rules for the people of the nation to live under.

When the hydroelectric dams were constructed in Canada in the James Bay region, the Cree lost most of their land.

Cree Indian Sun dancers (1893)

Today, there are around 200,000 Cree still living in Canada, with a small number living on a reservation in Montana in the United States.

Inuit

The Inuit made their home in the desolate and bleak regions of Alaska, Canada, Siberia, and Greenland. The way of life of these people has been greatly influenced by the weather conditions where they live.

Because it was difficult to find building material in the frozen Arctic Tundra, they made their homes from ice and snow. In the summer when the snow melted, they would use animal hides stretched over a wooden frame.

The Inuit name for home is ‘igloo.’

Because of the cold conditions, they needed warm clothing to survive. They wore animal skins and fur, and made jackets called ‘anoraks.’ Their clothes were lined with fur from animals that they hunted. These included foxes, rabbits, and polar bears.

GOKH, A Y 0075

Wednesday, December 1, 2021

R0457930569

The conditions did not allow the Inuit people to farm the land, so they lived off hunting the animals that they found around them. They made harpoons (spears) to hunt whales, walruses, seals and fish. In the summer, they would supplement their diet with wild berries. Their food was mainly fatty, which was ideal to combat the cold conditions.

To travel around, the Inuit's used sleds that were pulled by dogs. These dogs were bred from wolves especially for the task. The dog sleds were made of wood and whalebone, and the dogs were called Huskies.

Iroquois

The Iroquois lived in Northeast America and were made up of five tribes. The Seneca, Oneida, Onondaga, Cayuga and the Mohawk. The name Iroquois was given to them by the French, but the tribesmen called themselves Haudenosaunee, which translated means 'People of the Longhouse.' The British simply called them the Five Nations.

The Iroquois had a formalized system of government. The chiefs of each tribe would meet in a centralized council for major decisions to be made.

The people lived together in longhouses that were constructed using wood. The houses didn't have any windows and could be up to 100 feet long. Many families would live together in this accommodation.

The Iroquois farmed the land and grew crops such as squash, beans, and corn. The men of the villages hunted for wild game like beaver, turkey, deer, and rabbit. As with all of the Native American tribes, every part of the animal was used in some way or another. Nothing ever got wasted.

The men of the tribe shaved their heads, except for a strip of hair down the middle. The girls of the tribe would wear two braids in their hair if they were single and one if they were married.

A village was made up of several longhouses. Even though these were permanent structures, the villages would typically move to another place every ten years.

A trail connected the five nations that made up the Iroquois. It was called the Iroquois Trail.

The Iroquois invented the popular game of Lacrosse, which is still played today all over the world.

Navajo

The Navajo is one of the biggest Native American tribes. They lived in Utah, Colorado, New Mexico, and Arizona.

Navaho Warrior

They lived in a construction that was called a Hogan. These were houses in the shape of a dome with wooden frames and mud walls. The door of every Hogan faced to the east so that they could see the sunrise.

The Navajo farmed the land and hunted. They often kept herds of sheep and goats. Their main diet was mutton, fried cornbread and sometimes prairie dog.

The women of the Navajo were expert in weaving cotton and wool into blankets. Even today, Navajo rugs are in demand but can be extremely expensive.

The Navajo have very close links with the Apache. Today, the nation has the biggest Native American reservation in the United States. The capital city of the reservation is called Window Rock.

The language of the Navajo is so difficult to learn that during World War Two, it was used as a secret code.

Nez Perce

Today, there is a Nez Perce reservation situated in Idaho. This nation, however, once lived all over the states of Idaho, Washington, and Oregon.

At the end of the 1800s, many settlers from Europe began to arrive in the land of the Nez Perce. A treaty was eventually signed, which was later broken by the United States Government when gold was discovered. Prospectors moved in and took even more of the land.

The Nez Perce fought back against the arrival of the settlers. Under the leadership of Chief Joseph, they tried to escape into Canada but were caught and forced to surrender.

This nation lived in small villages that were usually near water. Like the Iroquois, they constructed longhouses, though in the summer they would follow the buffalo herds and live in tepees.

These people were famous for being fantastic horsemen and breeding fine horses.

They created both the Appaloosa horse breed and the Nez Perce.

Today, there are very few people that speak the Nez Perce language, and it will probably become extinct in the next couple of generations.

Nez Perce family

Osage

The Osage were a powerful Native American Nation that dominated much of the central United States. They lived in Missouri, Kansas, Oklahoma and Arkansas. Today, a lot of the Osage people live on a reservation in northern Oklahoma. During the last part of the 1800s, the Osage were forced to move from their land to make way for European settlers.

The Osage lived in wigwams and tepees, hunted local animals and farmed vegetables such as squash, beans, and corn.

A lot of the Osage became wealthy when oil was discovered on their reservation in 1894,

Today there are about 15,000 Osage left in the US.

Pueblo

The Pueblo Tribe is made up of 21 separate Native American clans that lived in New Mexico and Arizona.

Pueblo Terraced Housing

Much of the land occupied by the Pueblo was taken over by the Spanish. They forced the natives to become Catholic and gave them protection from the Navaho and Apache. The Pueblo grew tired of being treated as nothing more than slaves by the Spanish, and in 1680 revolted. They threw the Spanish out of their lands and kept them out for 12 years. However, when the Spanish took over again, they allowed the Puerto to keep their own religion.

The traditional homes of the Pueblo Native Americans are famous. They made multi-story houses of adobe clay and stone.

The Puebla constructed many roads between their villages. Some of these roads were built for religious purposes, and don't lead anywhere.

Seminole

The Seminole nation originally inhabited Northern Florida. With the arrival of more and more European settlers, they were gradually pushed out and moved to Southern Florida and Oklahoma.

The Seminole Nation was formed out of a collection of several other nations during the 1700s. They lived in cabins built with logs, but when they moved to Southern Florida, they lived in chickees. These were constructions with a raised floor, thatched roof, and open sides.

The Seminole men wore shirts with a belt and turbans on their heads. The women dressed in long skirts with short blouses.

The Seminole utilized the water in Florida to transport themselves. The built canoes out of logs to do this and hunted in the lakes and rivers for fish.

In an effort to keep their land, the Seminole fought a series of wars with the government of the United States. Although many Seminole resisted the government troops by hiding in the many swamps, eventually they were forced to move from their homeland to reservations situated in Oklahoma.

Seminole Family

Chickee is the Seminole word that means house. In Florida, many cities and rivers get their names from Seminole words. Chattahoochee (marked stones), Ocala (spring), and Hialeah (prairie) are examples.

Today, every spring, the Seminole have a traditional festival called the 'Green Corn Dance,' which is the most important event of their year.

Sioux

The Sioux Nation lived on the American Great Plains. They were made up of the Eastern Dakota Sioux, the Western Dakota Sioux, and the Lakota Sioux. The tribes were traditionally nomadic, and they followed the great buffalo herds around. They used the buffalo for food, clothing, housing, and tools. The lifestyle of the Sioux and the buffalo were intertwined.

Because they were constantly on the move, their homes could be easily taken down and rebuilt. They lived in tepees, which were constructed with poles and the hides of the buffalo.

Even though they ate a lot of buffalo meat, they also grew crops such as beans, squash, and corn. They also ate elk and deer. For the winter months, they dried out buffalo meat into 'jerky,' which could be stored and lasted a long time without decaying.

The Sioux were fierce warriors and excellent horsemen. They fought with bows and arrows and spears. One of their most famous medicine men was Sitting Bull.

The First Indian War

This war took place between 1675 and 1678.

The war was between English colonists and a group of Native American tribes. The prominent tribal leader was Metacomet, who was the chief of the Wampanoag nation. The English nicknamed him 'King Philip.'

During the war, two Native American tribes, the Mohegan and the Pequot, sided with the English. The war was fought throughout New England, Maine, Rhode Island, Connecticut, and Massachusetts.

The first 50 years after the arrival of the settlers, was relatively peaceful, but as more Europeans arrived, the local tribes saw that they were expanding rapidly and taking their land. The settlers broke many promises, and that is why the fighting began.

THE KING PHILIP WAR—A RAID ON THE SETTLERS.

The war started after three Wampanoag men were executed by the English. Both sides attacked each other over the course of the years, and many lives were lost.

However, with the arrival of more and more settlers, the outcome was inevitable.

During the conflict, about 600 English colonists were killed and 12 towns burnt to the ground. About 3000 Native Americans lost their lives. The tribes were eventually forced to concede even more land to the settlers.

The French and Indian War

This was a bitter and hard fought war that began in 1754 and ended in 1763. It was because of this war that the British took a lot of territory in North America.

This war was part of the struggle that was taking place in Europe between the French and the British. In North America, it lasted for seven years. Some Native Americans took sides with the British and some with the French.

ARRIVAL OF INDIAN ALLIES AT THE FRENCH CAMP.

In the short term, the British were the winners; the signing of the Treaty of Paris forced France to give up its influence in North America.

In the end, this war was one of the major causes that led to the American Revolution and eventual independence from Britain.

The Battle of the Little Big Horn

The Battle of the Little Big Horn was fought between the United States Army and several tribes that had joined together to fight the constant encroachment onto their land by settlers. The battle is also known as Custer's Last Stand.

The army had around 650 men, led by George Custer and Major Marcus Reno.

The tribes had several influential leaders that included Sitting Bull, Crazy Horse, and Lame White Man. There was a combined tribal force of 2,500 warriors from the Lakota Sioux, the Dakota Sioux, The Cheyenne and the Arapaho.

Sitting Bull

The battle took place in Montana on the banks of the Little Bighorn River.

The battle was fought after a treaty was broken by the US government. This was due to gold being discovered in the Black Hills. The US government wanted to take the Black Hills off the Dakota Sioux, but they refused. The army was sent to force the tribes off their land.

Custer didn't realize how many warriors were in the village that he attacked. He was given information that led him to believe that there was only a few hundred.

The army was overwhelmed by the numbers and Custer was killed along with all of his men.

Even though the Native Americans won the battle, they were unable to cope with the arrival of more and more soldiers and were eventually forced off their land.

Wounded Knee

The massacre at Wounded Knee took place December 29 at Wounded Knee in South Dakota. It is considered to be the last major conflict that took place between the United States Army and Native Americans. In the battle, more than 200 men, women, and children of the Lakota Sioux Nation were killed.

Troops at Wounded Knee

With more and more settlers pouring into America, the Native American tribes like the Lakota Sioux lost more and more land. Because the great herds of buffalo were now over hunted and killed more efficiently with rifles, food became scarce. Treaties by the US government had been broken, and land given by these treaties had been taken away.

The Native Americans formed a movement called the 'Ghost Dance.' The tribes believed that by practicing the Ghost Dance that the foreign invaders would go away.

With the death of Sitting Bull, the tension between the settlers and the tribes came to a head at Wounded Knee. A stray gunshot panicked the soldiers, and they opened fire. Hundreds of Native Americans were killed and 25 soldiers.

Crazy Horse

Crazy Horse was a Sioux Chief. He was born in South Dakota in 1840. He died in 1877. He was known for fighting against the US military.

In 1876, Crazy Horse led his braves against General Custer at the Battle of the Little Big Horn. Despite the victory, he surrendered to the military the next year and was killed trying to escape.

Geronimo

Geronimo was an Apache chief who was born in Arizona in 1829. He was thrown from a horse and died in 1909.

Mexicans killed his family, and Geronimo gathered a band together and set off to get revenge. During the next seven years, he led a series of attacks against Mexican villages.

When the Mexican-United States war ended, the US government tried to take control of the land of the Apache. Geronimo fought back, but eventually the Apache leader, Cochise signed an agreement. The Apache were moved to a reservation.

When the American government broke its promise, Geronimo began to raid American villages and Mexican villages. He used the US/American border to great effect to evade being captured. It became an obsession of the US Army to capture Geronimo and thousands of troops were sent to the area.

He was captured in 1886 and spent the rest of his life as a prisoner of war. Despite never being allowed to return to his homeland, he took on celebrity status and is today, one of the most famous Native Americans.

Sitting Bull

Sitting Bull was the leader of the Lakota Sioux Nation. He was born in 1831 in South Dakota. He died December 15, 1890.

When gold was discovered in the Black Hills and settlers began to arrive. Sitting Bull tried to scare them off, but it didn't work.

Sitting Bull saw the Battle of the Little Big Horn in a vision, and saw that General Custer was going to be defeated.

Sitting Bull and Buffalo Bill

The battle of the Little Big Horn is considered to be the greatest victory ever for Native Americans. However, it did have grave consequences.

After retreating to Canada, he was eventually captured in 1881. He was forced to live on a reservation.

Sitting Bull was involved in the Ghost Dance Movement and was killed in a shootout with American Police.

Sitting Bull worked for a while in Buffalo Bill's Wild West show. He was friends with Crazy Horse and Annie Oakley.

Sitting Bull is one of the most famous Native Americans. He is reported to have said. "I would rather die an Indian than live as a white man."

Facts and Trivia

The American city with the largest Native American population is New York.

The Vikings arrived in America a long time before Christopher Columbus. There is evidence that suggests they made contact with Native Americans 500 years before Columbus.

Many Native American words are now part of the English language. These include barbecue, chocolate, hammock, hurricane, potato, skunk, and toboggan.

Native Americans were the first people to make popcorn.

Native Americans did not use wheels. For transport, they used two poles with buffalo hide in the middle. These were often pulled by large dogs.

In America today, the most widely spoken Native American language is Navajo. There are more than 200,000 speakers.

Native Americans were the first people to make maple syrup. The technique is still used today.

Before the arrival of European settlers, the Native American population was practically disease free. Because they had no immunity, many of the indigenous population died from diseases such as typhoid, scarlet fever, smallpox, whooping cough, and influenza.

Epidemics over the years killed many Native Americans, and reached 80-90% of the population in the hardest hit areas.

Native Americans were not granted US citizenship until 1924.

How many things have you learned?

1 Why did European settlers call Native Americans, Indians?

2 What is a reservation?

3 What is the leader of a tribe called?

4 Who was killed at the Little Big Horn?

5 What was the 'Ghost Dance?'

6 How did Geronimo die?

7 Who was Sitting Bull?

8 What happened at Wounded Knee?

Thank you for Reading this Book

You can visit the English Reading Tree Page by clicking:

Visit Amazon's Keith Goodman Page on the Amazon site

Books in the English Reading Tree Series by Keith Goodman include:

1 The Titanic for Kids

2 Shark Facts for Kids

3 Solar System Facts for Kids

4 Dinosaur Facts for Kids

5 American Facts and Trivia for Kids

6 Christmas Facts and Trivia for Kids

7 Space Race Facts for Kids

8 My Titanic Adventure for Kids

9 Save the Titanic for Kids

10 Halloween Facts and Trivia for Kids

11 Discovering Ancient Egypt for Kids

12 Native American Culture for Kids

13 Meet the Presidents for Kids

14 The Universe and Stuff for Kids

15 The American Civil War Explained for Kids

16 The American Revolution Explained for Kids

17 The Planets for Kids

18 World War One in Brief for Kids

19 World War Two Explained for Kids

20 Bigger or Smaller for Preschool Kids

21 Opposites for Preschool Kids

22 Colonial America for Kids

23 Middle Ages Facts and Trivia for kids

24 The Cold War Explained for Kids

25 Planet Earth Explained for Kids

26 The Wild West and Stuff for Kids

27 The Great Depression and Stuff for Kids

28 Early American History for kids

CPSIA information can be obtained
at www.ICGtesting.com
Printed in the USA
LVHW041521030820
662267LV00005B/904

9 781520 502762